Children
and Divorce

....

Helping When Life Interrupts

Amy Baker

New
Growth
Press

www.newgrowthpress.com

New Growth Press, Greensboro, NC 27404
www.newgrowthpress.com
Copyright © 2012 by Amy Baker.

All rights reserved. No part of this publication may be reproduced,
stored in a retrieval system, or transmitted in any form by any means,
electronic, mechanical, photocopy, recording, or otherwise, without
the prior permission of the publisher, except as provided by USA
copyright law. Published 2012.

All Scripture quotations, unless otherwise indicated, are taken from
the *Holy Bible, New International Version*®, NIV®. Copyright ©
1973, 1978, 1984 by International Bible Society. Used by permission
of Zondervan. All rights reserved.

Scripture quotations marked ESV are taken from the *Holy Bible,
English Standard Version*® (ESV®), copyright © 2000, 2001 by
Crossway Bibles, a division of Good News Publishers. Used by per-
mission. All rights reserved.

Cover Design: Tandem Creative, Tom Temple, tandemcreative.net
Typesetting: Lisa Parnell, lparnell.com

ISBN-13: 978-1-938267-88-8
ISBN-13: 978-1-938267-27-7 (eBook)

        Library of Congress Cataloging-in-Publication Data
Baker, Amy, 1959–
  Children and divorce : helping when life interrupts / Amy Baker.
      p. cm.
  Includes bibliographical references and index.
  ISBN-13: 978-1-938267-88-8 (alk. paper)
  1. Divorce—Religious aspects—Christianity. 2. Children of di-
vorced parents—Religious life. I. Title.
  BT707.B35   2012
  248.8'46—dc23

                                                    2012026567

Printed in Canada

20 19 18 17 16 15 14 13   3 4 5 6 7

A divorced mother of three children wept as she told her support group how she found her daughter's journal lying open on her bed. "I didn't realize how depressed she was. She's written really dark things. She talks about taking pills and drifting off to sleep forever. I'm terrified she'll do it. I hid my Prozac and called her pediatrician for help. I feel so guilty. She's been saying for months that she hates her dad. I know I shouldn't let her talk like that, but after what he did to me, it feels good."

Next, a thirty-four-year-old mom who was working full time and going back to school shared about her ten-year-old son trying to take care of her. "I can see he worries about me. If I'm studying and don't sit down for dinner, he brings me a plate and tells me I need to eat. Now he's talking about getting a newspaper route so he can help pay the rent. He's just a kid. This is too much for him."

The man sitting next to her shared about his seven-year-old daughter playing with dolls. "When I asked her what she was playing, she explained that this was the mommy doll and this was the daddy doll. The mommy doll comes back home and kisses the daddy doll. Then they go inside, and the mommy doll kisses the baby and says, 'I won't ever leave you again.'"

As these single parents voiced their concerns in the Monday night group, it was clear that the aftershocks of divorce were still shaking their worlds. One twenty-two-year-old mother talked about the daily screams of her son when she dropped him off at daycare. "It breaks my heart to leave while he's crying, but I have to get to work, or I'll be fired. He loves Miss Tina and Miss Valerie, but he's terrified I'm not coming back."

What about Your Family?

Perhaps your life has been interrupted by divorce too, and you've observed similar things in your children. Do your children struggle with sadness and depression? Are they prone to outbursts of anger? Are they fearful and anxious about what will happen to them? Do they seem torn up with guilt due to loyalty conflicts, feeling as if they have to choose sides between you and your former spouse?

Perhaps it's not only your children who are experiencing powerful emotions. Do you often feel overwhelmed by sadness and depression? Do you notice anger welling up and spilling out in ways you immediately regret? Do you worry about the future, wondering whether you'll be able to pay the bills, whether you'll lose custody of the children in the next court battle, or whether you'll be able to make it on your own? Do you feel guilty because you secretly want your children to take your side against your former spouse?

The consequences of life interrupted by divorce keep coming, piling up destruction and damage. But there is hope. God has not left you by yourself. He promises that he will never leave you or forsake you (Hebrews 13:5). This minibook will remind you of the ways God is with you and your children, helping you despite the sad circumstances of your divorce. It will also help you direct your children to take their sadness, worries, guilt, loyalty issues, and anger to God.

Turn to God with Your Family's Broken Life

As you survey the rubble of your life, know that God is grieved by what has happened and wants you to turn to him for help. If Christ could take the utter ruin of the cross and turn it into the best thing that ever happened, he can reconstruct your life and the life of your children. If he could rise from the dead after three days, he can bring life back to you.

Jesus is not unsympathetic to your struggles. His advice is not an unemotional "Get over it." He is with you in your trouble and is willing to bear the weight of your burdens. He will walk with you through the aftermath of this disaster, and he will give you wisdom to help both you and your children. Neither you nor your children need to become one more statistic of brokenness. God can bring beauty out of ashes; he can lift the needy from the dust heap; he can make you and your children oaks of righteousness for the display of his splendor (Isaiah 61:3). God is at work most powerfully in the broken situations of life. He will not be distracted or diverted from his love for you. Even in the midst of the agony he experienced as he hung on the cross, Christ ministered to grieving people.

Maybe you feel heartbroken and alone, and you feel like God is far from you. With sadness, you may realize that you don't know what it's like to be close to God. You've been busy trying to take care of life on your own, without him, but perhaps now you are weary of going it alone. God might seem far away, but the truth is that even when you forget God, he has not forgotten you. Even when you try to move away from God, he does not move away from you. He is waiting for you to come to him with your burdens and ask him for the help you need.

Take a moment and think about what some of those burdens are. Certainly you have felt keenly the sins committed against you, but you've probably also experienced pain when you consider ways you've messed up. In the past, you may not have given much thought to verses expressing the failure of the entire human race to follow God and love him with all our heart, mind, soul, and strength (for example, Romans 3:23; Romans 3:10; Matthew 22:37), but perhaps you are starting to understand what the Bible means when it says that there is no one who does what is right. You know that your former spouse hasn't always done what is right and you know that you haven't either.

God sees both the wrongs that have been done to you and the ways that you have responded, and he invites you to come to him. Trust him to be your Rescuer and your Father. Tell him all of your troubles, admit your failure to do what is right, and ask him to be your Lord. He will heal your broken heart and freely forgive you for the ways you've messed up. He offers you the precious gift of eternal life and a relationship with him in which you will never be rejected. Be rescued by Christ and become God's child.

Just as you love your children, God loves his children. When you turn to the Lord in trust, he draws near. When you cry out to him, he parts the heavens and comes to your aid. When you ask for wisdom, he gives it generously. He forgives sins and pours his love into our hearts. He is truly a Father you can trust in times of need.

The same comfort and help you receive from the Lord can also be given to your children. As their parent, you have the privilege of communicating the Lord's help for sadness, fear, anger, loyalty conflicts, unmet desires, relationship problems, and guilt. You don't have to learn specialized techniques to do this because their hearts need the same truths and promises of God that sustain your own. While you will need to take into account your child's age and abilities,[1] their experience of fear, anger, resentment, and sadness is fundamentally the same as yours.

Of course, your child is not a carbon copy of you so some of the issues you see in your child will seem foreign to you. For example, your child may seem consumed with anger while you struggle with depression. At first glance, depression and anger can seem to be worlds apart, but they can both originate from being afraid or confused by what God is doing in our lives. While the way we experience circumstances and express our emotions can be different, we're all essentially alike. As you work through your own struggles, you'll be amazed at how the truths you learn also apply to your children.

Let's explore specifically some common struggles your children may face.

Sadness and Depression

Going through your divorce is likely the hardest thing that has ever happened to you. No matter what the reasons for your divorce, separating from the person whom you planned to build a life and a family with is utterly devastating. It's normal to feel sadness and rejection in this situation, and it's easy for that to turn into depression. Your children may feel rejected even if you've assured them the divorce is not their fault. Their little hearts are probably just as shattered as yours.

Jesus also knows what it is like to be overwhelmed with sorrow because of the rejection of those he loved. The night he was betrayed by a friend, he said, "My soul is overwhelmed with sorrow to the point of death" (Matthew 26:38). His betrayal by Judas was just the beginning of the treachery he experienced. This statement comes as Jesus agonizes over the horror of the cross he is about to face on behalf of those who betrayed him. He chose to suffer and be overwhelmed with grief to save us. When we meditate on the emotional anguish Jesus suffered by choice there should be no doubt that he truly is the only Man of Sorrows who can provide comfort for us and our children. The love displayed in his willing entry into our pain is unfathomable, and it guarantees that he completely understands our pain.

Think about how awful your own pain is and imagine choosing to endure it. As you suffer through this experience, you will come to know the love of your Savior more deeply as you cling to him. He is very near to you and your children, and knowing this can produce deep joy even in the midst of sorrow.

Psalm 31 is written from the perspective of someone who knows suffering. This person's eyes had grown weak with sorrow, and his soul and body were consumed with grief (vv. 9–10). Jesus quotes verse 5 of this psalm just before he dies, "Into your hands I commit my spirit," which displays amazing trust in God during a horrific experience. But Jesus fulfills this psalm not just by quoting it, but by becoming the refuge the psalmist seeks. God provides shelter for you and your children by giving you his Holy Spirit through Christ (v. 20). He has shown wonderful love to you by entering your pain (v. 21), and you can trust in him (v. 14) because of what he's done on the cross. You and your children can take refuge in him because you know how much he loves you by what he's done for you in Jesus.

Look for ways he has already begun to deliver you, and share this with your children. Remind them that Jesus knows how it feels to be rejected so they can trust him to listen to them. Together you and your children can begin to look for how God is helping and delivering you. Perhaps you received an unexpected gift that was just enough to pay the rent. Perhaps a new friend reached out to your child when she was hurting after your spouse deserted the family. These are not random acts of kindness; these are gifts from the good hand of God, especially planned for you. To be thankful for these things and recognize them as God's active presence in your lives will bring hope to your children that God has not forgotten or abandoned your family.

You may want to begin keeping a family journal of God's mercies during this hard time. Each child can take turns writing in it and one day of the week could be designated as a "Day of Remembrance" in which you review all the ways God has shown comfort and mercy to you and your children. As time passes, you and your children will have a growing record of God's faithfulness and care that will remind all of you how God has brought healing and rest despite (and in the midst of) sadness and grief.[2]

Fear

Again, you and your children may have much in common when it comes to fear. You might be afraid that you won't be able to pay the rent. Your children might be afraid that they won't be cared for. You might be afraid that you will fail without a partner. Your children are likely afraid that you might leave too.

Start by sharing with your children one verse, Psalm 56:3. This verse says, "When I am afraid, I will trust in you." Ask your children: what does it mean to trust in God when you are afraid? Remind your children that it means relying on the truth that God has promised to use his power and his love to do what is best for them. Go over this verse with them every night before they go to bed. Pray it with them as they are on the way out the door.

Remind your children that because God loves them perfectly, he won't let anything do permanent damage to them. Even if enemies on earth destroy their physical body, they can't destroy their soul; their soul is protected by the One whose name is "Power" (Mark 14:62 ESV). As his children, someday they will be with him in heaven and he will have wiped away every tear they've shed. Just as you wipe the tears from the cheeks of your children, he'll wipe the tears from the faces of his children. Encourage them every day to put all their trust in Jesus. If they have not yet turned to Jesus in faith and asked for forgiveness for their sins, use this opportunity to share with them how important it is to trust the Lord.

Sometimes when good things are snatched away from us through no fault of our own it feels as if nothing good is left. Joseph probably felt this way when he was torn away from his father and sold as a slave. (See Joseph's story in the book of Genesis, chapters 37–50.) In his situation, it was his resentful brothers who caused him to be "divorced" from his father and family members he loved deeply. Joseph had to live through many extremely difficult things as a result of his brothers' sinful actions. But Joseph discovered that even when other people do evil and intend to hurt you, God uses it for good (Genesis 50:20). God used Joseph to save entire nations from starving to death. God used Joseph to make sure his own family didn't starve (which is what would have happened to them all, including Joseph, if Joseph hadn't been taken to Egypt as a slave). God was keeping Joseph and his entire family safe for the future. He used Joseph to keep thousands of other children safe from starving. God doesn't always deliver us from fearful circumstances, but he enables us to find him and walk with him in the midst of them. He makes all circumstances work together for good for those who love him (Romans 8:28).

Sometimes what is best for you is unpleasant, hard, and even frightening, just like getting vaccinations is unpleasant and scary for your children. But because God is powerful and loves you, you can be confident that he'll do what is needed to make you like his Son. He won't give you a stone when you ask for bread. He won't give you a scorpion if you ask for eggs. God will give you good gifts when you ask (Luke 11:11–13). But just as you wouldn't give your children ice cream for breakfast if they asked for it, God may not give you the exact gifts you ask for. Just as you would give your children a nutritious breakfast instead of ice cream, God will always give you what is best for you.

You may want to post Psalm 56:3 on your fridge or your microwave to help your family remember who God is and that it is he that has all the power in your situation, not your circumstances or other people.

Explain that God sent Jesus to die so we could be forgiven and forever protected by him. When Jesus saves us he becomes our refuge and fortress and all who come to him are kept safe from the things that would harm us forever.

While it may take a lot of repetition before these truths sink in, be assured that as you remember them and pray them back to God, hope will grow stronger. These truths go deeper than the frightening situations you and your children face because of your divorce. When you belong to God, no circumstance can ever change your identity as a child of God. You belong to him for all eternity—he will never walk out on you. So as you comfort your children when they are scared, remind them that you are reflecting what God the Father does for his children. Encourage your children to go to him for comfort and help when they are afraid. Encourage them to pray to him for help.

As your children embrace these truths, as their understanding of God's love for them becomes more and more real, help them begin to show God's love to those around them. Experiencing God's love, always results in our love for others growing. We are able to love others because God has first loved us (1 John 4:19). Your children will find that as they focus on giving the same love to others that they have received from

God, their own fear will be lessened. Encourage them to love their parents, their siblings, and other children. Send them to daycare with a picture they've drawn to give to their caregiver, snacks they've helped make to share before naptime, or plans to be a helper by picking up the toys on the floor. Help your older children think of ways to be kind to others their age who seem to be struggling. They can sit with them during lunch, walk to class with them, text them to say hi, and so on. As you and your children remember God's love for you and then focus on showing love to others, you will find that gradually fear no longer dominates your thinking. God promises that perfect love casts out all fear. Knowing God's perfect love and sharing his love with others will replace fear with faith for you and your family (1 John 4:18).

Loyalty Conflicts

Perhaps the most difficult thing your children will face after your divorce is guilt because of a conflict in loyalty. After a divorce, virtually all children feel as though they must pick sides. Sadly, no matter which parent they choose, children will find they've also chosen to live with guilt. Your role as your child's parent is to *not* make them choose between you and your former spouse. Instead, you need to free them to love both of you.

As you seek to help your children in this area, it's likely that you will find yourself wrestling with wanting to capture your children's loyalty. You may find yourself justifying this desire to yourself or hiding it from others because you're ashamed to admit that you want your children to favor you over your former spouse. This is a common temptation that anyone in your situation is likely to face. Jesus knows how hard this is for you. You can turn to him with your desire to have your children love you best and ask him for forgiveness and help. He promises to help you and to give you a way to escape this temptation so that you don't burden your children with the guilt that comes from asking them to choose between you and your former spouse (1 Corinthians 10:13).

As you ask in faith (and keep on asking because this will be a constant struggle), God will empower you through his Spirit to have a forgiving love for your former spouse. That love will free your children from loyalty conflicts often created by parents' lack of love for each other. You can take the first step to bless those who curse you and love even your enemies—just as Christ did for us.

With God's help you can help lessen loyalty conflicts by encouraging your children to love your former spouse. Pray with your children each night, asking God to bless the absent parent and his or her new spouse if there's been a remarriage. Help your children pick out birthday gifts and special occasion presents for your former spouse. Have your children save their school papers to show the absent parent. If possible, sit with your former spouse when you go to your children's events, such as school programs, soccer games, and piano recitals. If that's not feasible, tell your children before the event that you want them to find their other parent right after the event. You can wait for the children in a predetermined place. Teach your children that Jesus' love is not exclusive. Jesus doesn't want them to love only Mom or only Dad. Jesus wants us to love everyone, even our enemies. *Of course, if your former spouse is abusive or your children are not safe when they are with him or her, you should use all available legal means to provide for their safety. This does not mean that you and your children are not called to love, but it does mean that they might need protection from the state and wise input from your church on what love looks like in your particular situation.*

Anger

Meltdowns, sullenness, temper tantrums, slammed doors, cold rejection, irritability, and impatience may all be part of your life after divorce. Like wounded animals, many of us lash out when we're hurt. You and your children may find anger boiling within you because vows have been broken, commitments have been disregarded, and people have been treated like throwaway objects. These are the things that make God angry too.

Anger at the wrong things that happen during a divorce—broken promises, harsh words, family turmoil, immature adults—is a right and appropriate response. If we are to properly reflect God's image, anger must be reflected in our response to wrong we see around us. As we reflect God's anger we must give careful attention to his instruction that we are not to sin in our anger (Ephesians 4:26). We must be careful not to return evil for evil.

When God looked at all the wrong things done in this world, he was angry. But God didn't lash out in his anger. Instead he sent his own Son to die on the cross and take the penalty for all the wrongs his people have done. God directed his anger in such a way that we have been redeemed, not consumed or hurt. Just as God forgave us in Christ, so too, we can imitate him and respond in a redemptive way to wrongs committed against us.

If meltdowns, sullenness, temper tantrums, slammed doors, cold rejection, irritability, and impatience have been the responses to wrong, encourage your child to go to Jesus for forgiveness and help. Share with them that repentance is God's way of giving us a new beginning. When we turn to God and ask him for forgiveness for Jesus' sake for the wrong things we have done, then our sins are wiped out and God sends times of refreshing (Acts 3:19–20).

Remind your child that God is not unjust and will not forget the wrongs you have suffered. But he alone will determine how to respond to the wrongs done to you and your child (Romans 12:17–21). Even though vengeance is his alone, God doesn't leave you and your children sitting on the sidelines. You have a role to play. Your family's role is to overcome evil with good. This will be difficult and you will need God's strength and power, but as you do so you will be following Christ. He returned good for evil by taking our punishment on the cross.

Remind your children that God is also angry when he sees wrongs being done. Then, after you have helped them see how God responded to our wrong by sending his Son to die, share Ephesians 4:32 with them, "Be kind to one another, tenderhearted, forgiving one another, as God in Christ forgave you" (ESV). Right after God tells us not to sin when we are angry, he instructs us to be kind and compassionate to one another, forgiving each other just as in Christ God forgave you.

What are some ways your children can be kind and compassionate in their separated family?

- By talking humbly and kindly to a parent whom they believe wronged God and them, gently explaining how they have been hurt and asking the parent to consider making changes.
- By being willing to forgive offenses rather than nursing them and becoming bitter.
- By praying and asking God to bless those who have wronged them.
- By patiently waiting for others to repent, rather than insisting change take place overnight.

Help your children practice being kind and compassionate in all areas of their lives, not just with family members. As they strengthen these qualities by practicing them with everyone in their lives, it will be less difficult to put them into effect with family.

Conclusion

You probably already know that children from divorced families have wounds. It's likely that their parents' divorce has brought some degree of betrayal, vulnerability, deception, and manipulation into their lives. Because of divorce, many children have been functionally left fatherless or motherless. But God sees their trouble; he considers their grief; he understands the way divorce interrupts life; and he takes it in hand.

He is the helper of the fatherless (Psalm 10:14). Even though your children have been victimized, they are able to be victors in Christ.

For both you and your children there is hope in our faithful God who sends his Spirit to live in the hearts of everyone who turns to him in trust and repentance. Naturally, you will face problems for which you have no immediate answers. Be quick to seek out counsel from your pastor or someone who will give you biblical, compassionate guidance. You will find that if you seek, ask, and knock, the door of wisdom will be opened. God generously gives wisdom to those who ask. God faithfully controls your circumstances so that you will not be tempted beyond what he will enable you to handle. By his grace and because of his great love, you and your children will grow to be oaks of righteousness, deeply rooted in our Savior's love and radiating his splendor.

Endnotes

1. You are already doing this in many ways by teaching your children according to their age and level of maturity. For example, when you tell your four-year-old it's time to get dressed, you probably go with him to help him pick out his clothes and put them on properly. Your teen, however, can do these things without your

help because you patiently helped and instructed him when he was younger. Now he is old enough to get dressed without assistance.

2. You will want to adapt these and the other suggestions in this minibook to suit the age and maturity of your children.

Simple, Quick, Biblical
Advice on Complicated Counseling Issues
for Pastors, Counselors, and Individuals

MINIBOOK
CATEGORIES

- Personal Change
- Marriage & Parenting
- Medical & Psychiatric Issues

- Women's Issues
- Singles
- Military

USE YOURSELF | GIVE TO A FRIEND | DISPLAY IN YOUR CHURCH OR MINISTRY

Go to **www.newgrowthpress.com** or call **336.378.7775** to
purchase individual minibooks or the entire collection.
Durable acrylic display stands are also available to house
the minibook collection.